Sausage Family
Palmwine Sounds

Copyright © 2024 Palmwine Publishing Limited Nigeria

All rights reserved. No part of this publica tion may be reproduced, distributed, or transmitted in any form or by any means, including photocopying, recording, or other electronic or mechanical methods, without the prior written permission of the publisher, except in the case of brief quotations embodied in critical reviews and certain other non-commercial uses permitted by copyright law.

Author- Palmwine Sounds

Illustrations by @chirose_illustrations
Chioma Rosemary Onyekaba - (Inner)
Kehinde Omotosho (Cover)

ISBN (Paperback)- 978-1-917267-08-3
ISBN (E-Book)- 978-1-917267-09-0

Published by Nubian Republic on behalf of Nucifera Analysis Limited Nigeria an Imprint of Palmwine Publishing Nigeria.

Email: info@palmwinepublishing.com

Address- UK: 86-90, Paul Street, London EC2A 4NE

Address-Nigeria: 1A Jos Road Bukuru, Plateau State, Nigeria.

www.palmwinepublishing.com
www.raffiapress.com
www.nuciferaanalysis.com

SAUSAGE FAMILY

About the Book

This book is a continuation of my "sausage series," delving deeper into the production department, a place I've previously praised for its positive work environment. However, a recent experience has brought to light the unethical behavior of a few individuals within the warehouse who seem to view it as their personal domain.

Through a combination of poetry and short stories, I'll explore the ethical dilemmas and biases these individuals exhibit. Despite this negativity, I want to reiterate that the production department itself remains a positive and enjoyable place to work for the majority of us.

The warehouse is still located in Leeds, West Yorkshire. Recent events have unfortunately portrayed me as someone with threatening behavior. It has also come to my attention that some colleagues may be conspiring to fabricate a criminal record for me. While I won't name names, it's important for my side of the story to be heard. This book is not driven by anger or hatred, but rather by disappointment and sadness.

TABLE OF CONTENT

Beauty --- 1
Yelling --- 4
Rudeness --- 4
Tears --- 7
Angels --- 8
Cats --- 9
Stubbornness --- 11
Forgiveness --- 13
Rights --- 13
Jah Guides --- 16
Wicked Game --- 17
The Wisest Man in Babylon --- 19
Chaos Show --- 21
Mental Health --- 23
Suspension --- 25
Ignorance 2 --- 26
Poetry --- 28

Sausage Family by Palmwine Sounds

Beauty

True Beauty Lies Within
The flesh is eye candy.
The heart defines beauty.
Beauty lies in character.

You may ask yourself why the first poem is called "Beauty." The female in this story, whom I shall call Ms. F, is truly beautiful; I even complimented her beauty once. But beauty does not define character or morals.

Let's begin with Ms. F. Ms. F has apparently been working in the warehouse from an early age, as both her mum and dad work there. Her mum is a sweet soul, from what I have seen. Her dad is also very happy and a motivating presence in the warehouse; he is currently a supervisor.

Ms. F tends to raise her voice, often targeting ethnic minorities in the warehouse, and feels she can get away with it. She has raised her voice at me a couple of times, which I chose to ignore. But on this particular day, she did it quite a few times, and I reacted by raising my voice back at her. She then ran to another team leader, who also yells a lot but won't fault her. This team leader is actually a sweet soul, just under pressure from upper management to meet targets. The team leader's department is not as automated as other departments.

I then went to speak to Ms. F's dad privately about the issue. Ms. F walked into the office during our private conversation,

Sausage Family by Palmwine Sounds

claiming she had the right to report me for yelling at her. Her dad offered to get her to apologize, but her attitude was unapologetic, and her mannerisms were rude, so I declined the offer. It would be more understandable if she were management.

Yelling

Don't yell at me.
I am who I am.

You know nothing about my background.
You know nothing about my struggles.

You feel that you are better than me.
To me, we are all the same in the eyes of Jah

Rudeness

Beauty equals rudeness.
I am also beautiful too.

Don't be impolite.
Bad mannerisms.

Be nice and smile.
You are beautiful.

Sausage Family by Palmwine Sounds

We beautiful have an advantage.
People treat us better just because.
Not fair, but I did not deal the deck.

A couple of days later, due to it being a bank holiday weekend, I submitted an informal grievance regarding her behavior. On the same day I filed the grievance and begged to take the rest of the week off, he spoke to the manager above him for approval. The following week, I brought in a sick note, as I was stressed out and had headaches. The same day I brought in the sick note, I happened to meet a female colleague on the bus. She complained about Ms. F's behavior, even coming to tears. I told her to be patient with me. This colleague is one of the most hardworking people I know. I would say she works harder than me. She is also an ethnic minority in the warehouse. The similarity between this female colleague and Ms. F is that both have newborn kids, so there should be a bond between them. I am one of the few people the female colleague talks to in the warehouse.

The day I submitted my grievance, another colleague overheard a plot to label me for threatening behavior against Ms. F, which could apparently land me with a criminal record. The heart of man is wicked; you want to forgive, but the plot behind your back is disheartening.

Other colleagues have also complained about her behavior when I started talking about what happened to others.

Sausage Family by Palmwine Sounds

Tears

Joyous tears I love to see.
Tears of pain break my soul.

Rasta man protects his own.
I cry silent tears with you.

Angels

Angels come in different forms.
Some watch over you spiritually.
Some manifest in the physical,
Protecting you from wickedness.

I was going to accept an apology and let the issue slide. I have a soft spot for females, having grown up mostly around them. I am someone who is in touch with his feminine side. Ask any female in the warehouse; I am soft-spoken to them. Beauty can also be wicked.

Cat

I wish I was a cat,
Feminine in nature,
Masculine combined,
Both male and female,
Strolling with pride,
Heads held high.

After my time off work, I did not receive any updates on my grievance, and the grace period for an update had passed. This same thing occurred with my previous grievance; I have to chase up for everything. A brief background about myself: my mum is the last female in a huge family, and she is stubborn, so I tapped a bit from that. I will fight for my rights to my last drop. The manager I submitted my grievance to is a good one. I just feel he does not have the heart to handle such issues, knowing the girl from a young age. It might sound weird, but I don't blame him. This one is really heavy.

Sausage Family by Palmwine Sounds

Stubbornness

Free the madness.
Madness is free.
Tap it like palm wine.

We want what we want.
We will find our way.
Don't test the stubborn.

We are called revolutionists.
We are called black sheep.
We are called prophets.

The same day of my return to work, the female colleague called me at about 10 PM, crying on the phone and complaining bitterly about Ms. F. I calmed her down and said I would organize a meeting on her behalf with the supervisors of the warehouse. I was already tired and had the morning shift. Then I made my grievance formal. It has to be taken seriously. I was ready to forgive and let it go, but some people do not learn. Another colleague told me they saw her get scolded, coming to tears. I don't know if it was for the same issue, but some tears are fake.

Sausage Family by Palmwine Sounds

Forgiveness

Not all deserve forgiveness.
Wickedness resides within.
A hard lesson is needed.
The hammer shall feast again.

A new character would now be introduced to the story: Mr. M. The first day I met Mr. M, it might sound weird, but I felt bad vibes from him. I assisted with some maintenance work as overtime on a Saturday, and his energy was not on the same wavelength as mine. It's hard to put into words. This is no evidence towards his character, just a thought I should mention. Mr. M was to handle my grievance against Ms. F. We first had to have the meeting with the female colleague, during which he tried to block me from accompanying her. She just stood in the room with two male supervisors, shedding tears and staying mute until I convinced Mr. M to let me in. He did not want to let me in until I showed that I knew my rights. When I went in, she laid her complaint. I would love to tell her story, but I feel it is not my story to tell. This should remain about me because I might mix her words in this story.

Rights

I may look unintelligent.
I may play foolish, dumb.
It's all part of my act
To discover truths.

Sausage Family by Palmwine Sounds

I may not be a lawyer.
I may not be a solicitor.
But I know basic rights.
Fight till the last drop of blood.

After the female colleague cried to management, Mr. M wanted to have my investigation done that same day, but I stood my ground and said I would want a union representative present for the meeting. He then agreed on the following week for the investigation to be carried out. After speaking to my union representative, I was advised to carry out the grievance with a union representative in the warehouse. I did not want to get the current union representative involved because he handles most of the family events at the warehouse, and I just had pity for him, thinking he would be emotionally attached. We then agreed that any colleague could tag along with me as a witness. But on arriving for the grievance, I was ambushed by a different grievance for threatening behavior by an unknown person, also handled by a supervisor. A colleague tagged along with me, and I said I would not have this grievance until mine was dealt with. This is my right. Another breach of rights again. My angel protected me. Supervisors are not trained to handle grievances. Throughout the week, Mr. M tried to shut me up when I was speaking to him so that other colleagues would not catch wind of the issue, which is another breach of basic human rights. Mr. M was trying to play the wicked game. I never initiate the wicked game; I am a man of peace. I would pray to Jah first and fight the spiritual battle. I am a huge believer in the phrase, "All battles happen in the spiritual realm before they manifest in the physical." Each to his own, not forcing my spirituality on anyone. So I prayed to God about the issue and let Him steer the wheel. This situation is too huge for me to handle, so I laid it at Jah's feet. Mr. M, acting like the wisest man in Babylon, acted cunning to protect his own because his daughters are friends with Ms. F. But I thought I was meant to be treated fairly and equally, without discrimination. They tried to get me fired because if I had confessed during that meeting to yelling at her, I would have been given a dismissal, as the company would paint me as a threat to push me out, and there would be nothing I could do about it. So for pointing out wrongs, they want to paint me as a threat. I shall stand and fight.

Jah Guides
Let Him steer the wheel.
Just enjoy the journey.
It's smooth and bumpy.
Jah on the wheel, cruise.

Wicked Game

Want to play the wicked game?
Remember, Your deck deals only physical damage.
Mine deals both physical and spiritual.
I may appear to be losing at the start,
But my spiritual cards are just powering up.
Spiritual damage deals physical damage too.
Jah plays the game on my behalf.
I would never dabble in wickedness.

Sausage Family by Palmwine Sounds

The Wisest Man in Babylon

Jah's children will always be smarter.
The wisdom of the Father flows within.
Tapping directly from the Creator,
Babylonians shall all look stupid.

After that whole incident, my temper was up. I went home and did the same thing I did to get attention to my previous grievance: messaging members of head office, including the CEO of the company. Apparently, I sent 28 emails, including some poems I composed in the heat of the moment, some of which are included here. I also sent a copy of "God Bless Women" to prove I am not a threat, and "Life and Death" to show my views on life and death. Not going to lie, it was intense. A Rasta man's anger is pure and true.

Sausage Family by Palmwine Sounds

Chaos Show

Yanga on bassline,
Trouble on percussion,
Shakara on horns,
Wahala on the keys,
Angry Lion on the mic.

The tail has been touched.
Consequences are unpredictable.

Lights, camera, action.
Hope you enjoy the show.

After I got a reply from management, they sent me a link to contact regarding mental health, so they know I am mentally unstable. Battling two battles in the same warehouse at once. But they are painting me as a threat. I also filed a formal grievance against Mr. M.

Mental Health

My emotions are in shambles.
A soldier of Jah vs. an army.

How long can I stand my ground
Till justice and the hammer feast?

I shall not waver.
I shall not step back.

The next day, as soon as I started my shift, I was summoned upstairs by my union representative. I was put on paid suspension by the manager of the warehouse pending investigation into some of the poems I sent, which may be perceived as threats, but were not threats from my end. They were just poetic facts.

Sausage Family by Palmwine Sounds

Suspension

A bit of relief.
Bold face rest.
Tears flow down,
Soften the blow.

I was coming down with the flu, so I was a bit happy.

The same day, I received an email confirming my grievance meeting for the following week. You have to show a bit of madness to get what you want sometimes. Management always pushes me to the extreme. During the meeting, the manager claimed ignorance, stating he was on holiday during the whole process, even though he was the one who gave the go-ahead to give me the rest of the week off as holiday. But I also want to believe he is a good guy, just protecting himself. He has always been friendly and cheerful with me. But that does not mean he should act ignorant, though I understand. This same manager acted ignorant during the previous case in Sausage Management.

Sausage Family by Palmwine Sounds

Ignorance 2

I understand your ignorance.
Protect your integrity and virtue.
But in turn, you call me a fool,
Not directly, but emotionally.

But I still understand.
Would I do the same?
I am not in your shoes,
So I would never know.

After the meeting, upon getting home and resting for a bit, I received an email from management not for threatening behavior, but for sexualizing women. They handpicked a few poems from "God Bless Women" and "Life and Death," leaving behind the context of the books. A grievance was put forward by the whole of head office management.

Please, readers, I urge you to get a copy of both books and be the judge. Using a poet's words that come from love and appreciation against him is different. This hurts. Poetry comes from emotion, and my love has been threatened. Case in point, pick out poems from "Songs of Solomon" in the Bible; Solomon can be painted as sexualizing women.

Poetry

Poems bring me peace.
Poems bring me comfort.

Poems express my emotions.
Poems express my thoughts.

Poems show my appreciation.
Poems show my love.

I am just disappointed with management in Production for acting like this. I want to be forgiven, but they keep pushing. This is wrong on a different level. I feel threatened for pointing out the truth. As soon as the investigation is over, I will begin planning my exit. They have succeeded in making the workplace hostile towards me. I am a threat to the Family..

www.ingramcontent.com/pod-product-compliance
Lightning Source LLC
Chambersburg PA
CBHW070939180426
43192CB00039B/2387